Truc Handbook

J. J. Keller
& Associates, Inc.
Since 1953

©2005

J. J. Keller & Associates, Inc.
3003 W. Breezewood Lane
P. O. Box 368
Neenah, Wisconsin 54957-0368
Phone: (920) 722-2848
FAX: (920) 727-7455
http://www.jjkeller.com

Printed in the U.S.A.
Second Printing, February 2008

Due to the constantly changing nature of government regulations, it is impossible to guarantee absolute accuracy of the material contained herein. The Publisher and Editors, therefore, cannot assume any responsibility for omissions, errors, misprinting, or ambiguity contained within this publication and shall not be held liable in any degree for any loss or injury caused by such omission, error, misprinting or ambiguity presented in this publication.

This publication is designed to provide reasonably accurate and authoritative information in regard to the subject matter covered. It is sold with the understanding that the Publisher is not engaged in rendering legal, accounting, or other professional service. If legal advice or other expert assistance is required, the services of a competent professional person should be sought.

LIBRARY OF CONGRESS CATALOG CARD
NUMBER: 2005924283
ISBN: 1-59042-667-3
CANADIAN GOODS AND SERVICES TAX (GST)
NUMBER: R123-317687

17-ORS

TABLE OF CONTENTS

You and the public

Your job, the future of the company you work for, and the future of the overall trucking industry all depend on good public relations. In many cases, laws and regulations which restrict truck operations came about because of public pressure and dissatisfaction with the way in which some drivers operate their equipment. Or the occurrence of a single serious accident that could have been avoided led to a demand for new restrictions. No industry can afford to be insensitive to the impact of its operations on the public if it is to continue to prosper. Every company must accept the responsibility not to act in a way that endangers or inconveniences the public.

The purpose of this part of your handbook is to make you aware of the importance of your role as a professional driver. One definition of public relations is: "To do the things by which you earn public good will and esteem, and then see that you get it." Good public opinion doesn't just happen; it has to be earned.

Of all the employees in the trucking industry who can do a public relations job, you are in the most strategic spot. You are in direct contact with the public. You meet them on the streets and highways; you drive through their towns and past their homes and businesses. Some of this "public" might be your shipper or a member of the state legislature. Their opinions affect laws that hinder or help you and your company. You, as a professional driver, have the key to form the opinion of the public toward the trucking industry and truck drivers.

Your conduct behind the wheel is noticed by more people than any other phase of trucking industry operations. Realistically speaking, you often are the only representative of your company that a customer sees, so your behavior sets the tone for how your company is perceived by that customer and the public in general. What can you do as a truck driver to create and maintain better public relations? Following are some tips and driving behaviors to keep in mind.

Physical and mental condition: Your physical and mental condition plays an important part in your attitude and safe driving practices. You need adequate rest to be alert when you are behind the wheel. If you begin to feel tired, stopping for a short rest can significantly increase alertness and may prevent an accident. You must maintain good health in order to be medically qualified as a commercial motor vehicle (CMV) driver. Work on developing an attitude that allows you to be tolerant of other highway users so that anger won't outweigh your good judgment in a hazard situation.

Your personal appearance: You can gain or lose respect by how you look — it's as simple as that. In this case, people will judge "the book by its cover." Keep as neat and clean as possible — if your company provides uniforms, wear them. You will look good and feel better! Clothing and footwear that are in good condition are safer too. An unkempt looking driver simply does not promote a professional image.

Courtesy: Courteous habits are noticeable and carry a lot of weight in how you are perceived by the public. Above average courtesy is expected of you — the name of your company is right on the truck. Courtesy goes hand in hand with safety; finally driving courteously will lessen wear and tear on your disposition, and you'll feel better.

Following distance: The most frequent complaint against truck drivers is tailgating, especially by drivers of passenger cars. It is also a frequent cause of accidents. Never follow another vehicle at a time interval of less than 4 seconds at speeds over 40 mph under good road conditions. To check your following time, when the vehicle ahead passes a fixed point, start counting 1001, 1002, 1003, 1004. If you reach the specified point before you get to 1004 you are following too closely. And remember to stretch out that following time when there are adverse road or weather conditions.

Caravanning: When following another truck, always leave plenty of space between your unit and the one ahead so that a faster vehicle can pass and return to the right lane safely between the two units. Maintain this distance, or even increase it, if traveling with other vehicles from your company.

Ascending grades: Keep well to the right. If a climbing lane for slower traffic is available, use it. Do not pull out to pass another vehicle, even if it is safe, unless you are going at least 5 miles per hour

You and the public 5

faster and then only if you will not obstruct other traffic. On two-lane roads, pull over at the top of a hill if it is safe to do so, or ease up and let any accumulated traffic pass before you let your speed build up on the downgrade.

Rendering assistance: Follow any company policy that is in effect on stopping to assist at an accident scene or other emergency. Don't stop if authorities are present, or others have the situation under control. And if you do stop, park your unit where it will not obstruct other traffic. Take steps to protect the scene against further accidents. Always report any help you render during your trip. When your assistance is no longer required, you can resume your trip.

First aid training: First aid training is desirable. There are often occasions when you can be of help to injured people and perhaps save a life. You must be properly trained, however, in order to know what to do and how to do it. Local Red Cross agencies offer first aid training, if you are interested in getting some for yourself. Such knowledge also comes in handy at home.

Parking: When you park your vehicle, do it so you don't pin in another vehicle. Don't park where you will block the sight of stores, shops, driveways or the roadway. Be considerate of where you park your rig at night if your engine is running so as not to disturb people who are sleeping.

Stopping: Make safe, gradual stops and give drivers behind you adequate warning. Sudden stops increase the danger of being hit from behind. Whenever possible, make necessary traffic stops in the right lane to avoid blocking traffic unnecessarily. If you must stop on the open highway, get as far off the road as you safely can.

Going through towns: Always remember that a big truck appears to be going faster than it actually is to casual observers. Avoid criticism by observing speed limits religiously and driving carefully. Don't crowd other traffic. To minimize noise in built-up areas, drive with a light throttle and avoid using the engine brake or revving the engine. Don't use air horns unless necessary.

Intersections: Blocking intersections is illegal and discourteous. Avoid stopping beside another truck at a traffic signal so that traffic behind will be bottled up when the light turns green. Don't use the size of your vehicle to bluff your way through intersections. Stop if necessary, and let the other driver go first.

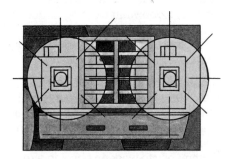

Headlights: Use high beams as much as possible, but remember that when approaching an oncoming car on a curve or at the crest of a hill, lower your lights before they hit the other driver's eyes. When a car has just overtaken you, drop your lights onto low beam until there is enough distance between you and the other vehicle so that the lights won't be a problem for that driver.

Off-duty activities: Probably more than any other group, professional drivers can be adversely affected by their off-duty activities. Be sure that you get enough rest so you will be ready when you are called for your next trip. If you have been awake for a long time, a nap can significantly improve your alertness. Avoid the excessive use of alcohol and don't use illegal drugs.

Drinking of any alcoholic beverage within 4 hours of going on-duty or driving is prohibited by federal regulation. Avoid loud and boisterous conduct in restaurants or other public places — remember your role as a representative of the trucking industry at all times. If you wear clothing or accessories that identify you, be particularly careful that your off-duty activities do not reflect adversely on you, your company, or the trucking industry.

General consideration: Treat drivers of other vehicles as though members of your family were riding with them. We hope that the suggestions given here will stimulate further thought, and encourage you as a member of the professional driver's community to work on building a reputation in the eyes of the public as true professionals.

Safe driving rules

Following you find some very basic "rules" to keep in mind when you are behind the wheel of your CMV. If there's any doubt, play it safe. Do not take chances under any circumstances. To arrive safely is far more important than to arrive on time.

You need to be in good physical condition to remain alert while you are driving and to perform your duties safely and efficiently. A driver who reports for work ill, fatigued or showing evidence of consumption of alcohol or illegal substances won't be permitted to work and may be subject to testing requirements and/ or disciplinary procedures. If you become ill or unduly fatigued on the road, you should stop at the first safe place. If your trip will be delayed more than an hour, notify your carrier and request relief.

You must comply with the hours of service limits of the Federal Motor Carrier Safety Regulations (FMCSR) at all times.

Report for work promptly when you are notified of a trip. That way you will have adequate time to check your equipment and be able to leave in time to avoid the need for excessive driving speed.

Federal regulations prohibit the possession of alcoholic beverages in a commercial motor vehicle except as a part of a documented shipment. A driver found with alcoholic beverages on the truck for personal use can be put "out of service" for 24 hours by the authorities and may also be subject to disciplinary action.

Federal regulations prohibit a driver from possessing, using, or being under the influence of any illegal drug or other substance likely to adversely affect his/her ability to drive safely. Drivers whose actions indicate they are using an illegal substance can be subject to drug testing under the "reasonable suspicion" provisions of the FMCSR or similar provisions of state laws.

Federal law also requires CMV drivers to report convictions for traffic violations, other than parking, within 30 days of receipt to the motor carrier and to the state in which the driver is licensed. Failure to report will subject the driver to a federal penalty up to $3750 and may result in disciplinary action.

Chronic traffic violations by a driver or complaints about driving behavior or unsafe or discourteous conduct may result in disciplinary action.

Drivers convicted of violations involving alcohol and drugs while on duty are subject to disqualification under the FMCSR.

Drivers must comply with company rules, applicable provisions of the FMCSR and the laws of the states, cities and towns through which they operate.

Every driver must have the appropriate type of Commercial Drivers License (CDL) for the type of equipment being operated and appropriate endorsement(s) for the types of cargo to be transported and/or equipment to be driven.

Knowledge of routes is very important to safety. A driver who is dispatched over an unfamiliar route should take extra care to guard against unexpected hazards.

Speed

Your speed should never be faster than a rate consistent with existing speed laws, traffic and weather conditions. Posted speed limits on the highway and in towns and cities must be obeyed at all times.

Speed should be reduced to a point that will enable you to stop within the distance you can see ahead at night and when fog or other conditions restrict visibility.

When traction and visibility are reduced by rain, snow, ice, or similar conditions, your speed should be reduced. Never forget that the posted speed limits apply only when conditions are favorable.

Federal regulations prohibit the use of radar detectors or other devices designed to detect speed limit enforcement. In addition to any penalties under the law, violations may subject you to company disciplinary action.

Right-of-way

Do not attempt to exercise the right-of-way; always let the other driver go first. Above all, never use the size of your vehicle to assert your right-of-way. Keep to the right except when overtaking slow-moving vehicles or when getting into position to make a left turn. This rule should also be adhered to on dual highways and one-way streets unless otherwise posted.

Be ready to yield to drivers who may pull out in front of you from side streets, at interchange ramps, private and public driveways or similar places. When entering a main thoroughfare from a side street, alley, driveway, garage, terminal yard, or buildings; make a full stop before entering any crosswalk. When the way is clear, you can then pull into the crosswalk, if necessary, to check traffic in the street before entering.

Emergency vehicles such as fire trucks, police cars and ambulances always have the right-of-way when they give warning with sirens or warning lights. On the approach of such vehicles, pull as far to the right as safely possible and wait until they pass. If you can't pull to the right, stop where you are and let them pass you.

Never break a funeral procession. And remember that military convoys in close formation have the right-of-way.

Following distance

On the open highway in good weather, maintain a following distance of 1 second per 10 feet of vehicle length to leave enough room for a safe stop in an emergency. Never follow another vehicle too closely to try to force that driver to speed up or get out of your way. Under the FMCSR, following too close is a "serious" traffic violation. Two convictions for serious traffic violations within a three year period will result in a 60-day disqualification.

Remember to increase following distances when roads are slippery due to rain, snow, ice, loose dirt, mud or the like. These conditions increase stopping distances 3 to 12 times.

On two-lane roads, always follow at a distance which will permit a faster driver to pass and return to the right lane easily and safely.

Keeping a safe following distance is not intended to keep you from passing slower traffic when you can do so safely. If you catch up to pass a slower vehicle and find you cannot do so, drop back to a safe following distance and wait for a better opportunity.

Passing

Passing should be attempted only where it is legal to do so and when you have adequate clearance to complete the pass without racing and without personal risk or creating a hazardous condition for others.

Signals should be given to indicate a change of lane both when pulling out to pass and when returning to the right-hand lane after the pass is completed. The required signal should be given for at least 100 feet before any actual change of lanes.

Signaling is only an indication of intention. It does not give you any right-of-way privilege or any guarantee that you can change lanes safely. You must check traffic conditions carefully and change lanes only when it can be done safely and without unduly interfering with other traffic

Size up the entire situation before passing. Look for side roads and driveways the vehicle you are passing might turn into, or from which a vehicle might pull out in front of you. Sound your horn if necessary. Flashing your headlights is not a legally-recognized warning signal. Return to the right-hand lane as soon as you can do so safely.

Don't be too quick to pass a driver whose actions are erratic or uncertain. That driver could be lost, be having mechanical trouble, be affected by alcohol or drugs, or may take an unexpected action that could cause an accident. Whenever you are passing, be ready to sound the horn if you need to do so.

On two-lane roads, never attempt to pass when you are approaching the top of a hill, a curve, intersection, side road, bridge, railroad crossing, or any place where you do not have a clear view of the road ahead, or where you cannot see traffic approaching from either side, whether or not there is a marked no-passing zone.

Stopped buses or street cars should be passed in accordance with local traffic regulations. Use utmost care when passing such vehicles.

Be alert for school buses and be ready to make a safe stop if necessary. You must comply with local school bus stop laws at all times. Many states require a stop in urban and residential areas, as well as on the open highway. Most states do not require you to stop if you are on the opposite side of a divided highway from the bus. When stopping, you should give as much warning as you can to traffic behind you.

Do not attempt to pass more than one vehicle at a time. If you try to pass a line of traffic you may find yourself in a position where you cannot return to the right lane safely when you need to do so.

On multiple-lane highways avoid blocking traffic when you pass. Don't try to pass unless you can maintain a speed difference of 5 miles per hour over the slower vehicle. On highways with three or more lanes of traffic in one direction, avoid using

the extreme left lane. On many such highways
trucks are not allowed to operate in the left lane by
posted regulation.

Being passed

When you are being passed by another vehicle,
keep well to the right and, if necessary, reduce
your speed a little to facilitate safe passing. Never
speed up to prevent another driver from passing
you. To do so is to create an unnecessary hazard
and invite unfavorable criticism of the trucking
industry and yourself.

Do not attempt to signal the driver of an overtaking
vehicle that it is safe to pass. This practice is prohibited by Department of Transportation (DOT)
regulations. To give such a signal would transfer
part of the responsibility for safe passing from the

other driver to you. In the event an accident would occur after you gave such a signal, you and the company could be held jointly liable for damages.

Be alert for a driver who tries to pass in an unsafe place. Don't try to block the attempt, but be ready to do anything that may be necessary to avoid being involved in an accident. At night, dim your lights after you have been passed to avoid creating objectionable glare in the other mirror.

Meeting other vehicles

Always keep to the extreme right when meeting an oncoming vehicle. At night dim your headlights when within 500 feet of an oncoming driver regardless of any action the other driver may take.

If you see a vehicle approaching on your side of the road, slow down; pull as far to the right as safely possible, and stop. Never, under any circumstances, pull to the left to try to avoid an oncoming vehicle in your lane.

Stopping and parking

Stopping or parking on the open highway should be avoided whenever possible. Stopping on the shoulder of a high-speed limited access highway is particularly dangerous and is usually prohibited by law except in an emergency situation.

If it's necessary to park on the highway, you should pull the unit as far to the right as possible, completely off the traveled portion of the road if at all possible.

Whenever it is necessary to park outside of city limits, set out emergency warning signals in accordance with DOT regulations, unless the unit is at least 10 feet away from the nearest part of a main traveled roadway. Set out emergency warning signals even in built-up areas if their use will help promote the safety and convenience of other highway users.

When parking, apply the parking brake and put the transmission in the lowest forward gear (or reverse) after shutting down the engine. If you are driving a vehicle with a two-speed or three-speed axle, put the axle in low range. Never use the trailer hand valve or tractor protection valve to hold a parked unit.

If a curb is available, turn your front wheels toward it when parking on the level or if you are headed downhill. If you are headed uphill, turn front wheels away from curb.

Avoid parking on steep grades. If such parking is unavoidable, you may have to block one or more wheels to prevent a roll-away.

Excessive idling wastes fuel, is hard on the engine, and is restricted in some localities as an air pollution control measure. If you are not in an area that has a law about idling, as a general rule do not leave the engine of a parked vehicle running for more than a 3-5 minute cool-down except:

    a.   When temperatures are so low that restarting the engine would be unduly difficult; or,

    b.   The engine is needed to operate auxiliary equipment.

Use of emergency warning devices

When you have to stop on the highway or the adjacent shoulder for any reason other than a normal stop, emergency warning devices must be used as required by the FMCSR.

You should know where the emergency warning devices are stored on the vehicle and must be able to retrieve them and set them up at night as well as in daylight.

For maximum effectiveness, reflective triangles should be placed at right angles to approaching traffic so that the surface will reflect in the headlight beams of oncoming vehicles. They should be placed in the center of the lane occupied by the stopped unit.

To provide adequate warning, reflective triangles must be set out at the prescribed distances. Pace off the distances as indicated below, based on $2\frac{1}{2}$ feet (30") per pace.

Immediately upon stopping activate the vehicle's four-way flashers. Leave them operating while you set out the reflective triangles. That has to be done as soon as possible, but no matter what within 10 minutes.

On a roadway carrying two-way traffic, set out reflective triangles as follows:

a. One on the traffic side of and 10 feet (approximately 3 meters or 4 paces) from the stopped commercial motor vehicle in the direction of approaching traffic;

b. One at 100 feet (approximately 30 meters or 40 paces) from the stopped commercial motor vehicle in the center of the traffic lane or shoulder occupied by the commercial motor vehicle and in the direction of approaching traffic; and

c. One at 100 feet (approximately 30 meters or 40 paces) from the stopped commercial motor vehicle in the center of the traffic lane or shoulder occupied by the commercial motor vehicle and in the direction away from approaching traffic.

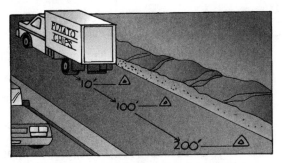

On a one-way roadway or divided highway, place reflective triangles as follows:

a. One warning device at a distance of 200 feet (approximately 60 meters or 80 paces) and

b. One warning device at a distance of 100 feet (approximately 30 meters or 40 paces) in a direction toward approaching traffic in the center of the lane or shoulder occupied by the commercial motor vehicle.

c. One warning device at the traffic side of the commercial motor vehicle within 10 feet (approximately 3 meters or 4 paces) of the rear of the commercial motor vehicle.

If the view of the unit is blocked by a hillcrest, curve or other obstruction to view, the warning signal required shall be placed in the direction of the obstruction to view a distance of 100 feet to 500 feet from the stopped commercial motor vehicle.

SOME SPECIAL CONSIDERATIONS ABOUT
EMERGENCY WARNING DEVICES

a. Avoid leaving four-way flashers on for long
    periods. Doing so can run down the bat-
    tery and keep you from restarting.

b. Six fusees or three liquid-burning flares
    are acceptable warning devices with which
    a vehicle may be equipped. Flame-produc-
    ing signals must be kept in operation for as
    long as the vehicle is stopped and they
    must be extinguished and removed from
    the roadside before you resume travel.

c. Fusees can cause severe burns. Be sure
    you know the correct technique for lighting
    them. Avoid looking into the glare.

d. Liquid burning flares, fusees, oil lanterns,
    or any signal produced by a flame must
    not be carried on any CMV transporting
    Division 1.1, 1.2, 1.3 (explosives) hazard-
    ous materials; any cargo tank motor vehi-
    cle used for the transportation of Division
    2.1 (flammable gas) or Class 3 (flammable
    liquid) hazardous materials whether
    loaded or empty; or any commercial motor
    vehicle using compressed gas as a fuel.

e. Never attach a lighted fusee to a vehicle.

f. Never use fusees or pot torches in an area
    where there may be leaking flammable liq-
    uids or gases.

Curves

Curves should always be
negotiated at speed consistent with the sharpness of
the curve, the available
sight distance and current
road, weather, and traffic
conditions. Reduce speed
to 5-10 mph below the
posted speed before entering any curve.

Posted advisory speed
signs show a maximum safe
speed for cars, but that speed may be too high for
your equipment.

Curved ramps at highway interchanges are particularly dangerous. As a general rule you should
reduce your speed 5-10 mph below any posted
ramp speed. Be especially alert and slow down at
ramps on which the curve gets progressively
sharper as you enter them.

When negotiating a curve on the open highway,
remember to stay entirely in your own lane. Don't
swing wide or cut short across adjacent lanes. If
going into the next lane is unavoidable, watch
other traffic and be ready for any problems.

Turns

Signal and get in the proper lane for the turn well in advance. That means left turn next to the center lane and right turn from as close as possible to the right-hand edge of the road, curb, or parked vehicles to keep traffic from trying to pass on the "turn side." The exception is tandem left turn lanes.

Signal well in advance — one block or 100 feet, whichever is less, in city traffic; 500 feet or more on the open highway. Make turns slowly.

Never turn or change lanes without being sure the way is clear. Turn your head to check traffic as well as using the mirrors. Continue checking traffic while turning.

Avoid situations where you might have to stop in mid-turn.

Remember to allow for off-tracking. The rear wheels of any vehicle follow a shorter path than the front wheels when turning. On right turns, try to keep the right side of your unit within 4 feet of the right edge of the road, or parked vehicles, to physically block any driver who might attempt to pass on the right. When necessary to clear the corner, pull across the intersecting street and then turn hard to keep the right side blocked off.

Extreme care is necessary when a right turn cannot be made from a position close to the right edge of the road. When making turns at places other than intersections, remember that other drivers are quite likely to be caught off-guard by your maneuver. Give them plenty of warning and check traffic carefully.

Safe backing

Whenever possible plan the route to avoid the need for backing. Avoid backing out into traffic. Responsibility for safe backing is always that of the driver, even when a helper is used. When a helper is used, that person should stand in a location visible to you and where he/she has a good view of the path of travel. If you cannot see the helper, stop and ascertain the helper's whereabouts before continuing.

You should get out and physically check the path of travel before and during backing. If you are backing a long distance, or into a tight spot it might be necessary to stop at intervals and recheck the travel path.

If you have to back across a sidewalk, or if you are backing in areas where pedestrians are likely to be present, lightly sound your horn occasionally as a warning.

Spotting vehicles for loading or unloading

When opening the swing-back doors before you back into the dock, be sure those doors are properly secured so they will not come loose and strike an adjacent vehicle or other object. Generally, roll-up doors shouldn't be opened until the vehicle has reached the dock. Be alert for falling freight (see Personal Safety section).

When you will be leaving a trailer at a dock, be certain to block the wheels. If an air-suspension trailer is left alone at a dock, the air in the suspension system should be exhausted to prevent the trailer from moving during loading or unloading. If the dock is

equipped with a mechanical restraint system, check for proper securement if it's possible.

Before pulling away from a dock, physically check to make sure that all people and equipment involved in loading or unloading are safely clear.

Before leaving a dock equipped with a mechanical restraint system, go back and physically check that the restraint mechanism has released, if there is room to do so. The signal system may give a false indication. If the restraint has not released, pulling away from the dock will cause major equipment damage.

Hooking and unhooking tractor trailers

Following are step by step guidelines for hooking up and unhooking tractor-trailer units.

HOOKING UP

1. Make sure fifth wheel jaws are fully opened.

2. Make sure fifth wheel is tilted back to avoid body damage when tractor backs under trailer.

3. Block semitrailer wheels or make sure brakes are locked. If necessary for safety, use both methods to keep the trailer stationary.

4. Before starting to back under a trailer, make sure brake hoses and light cords are clear and won't be damaged.

5. When hooking up, back under the trailer slowly. Check its height to avoid damage. If you are driving an air-suspension tractor, be sure the unit is at normal ride-height before you attempt the hook-up. Back the tractor as squarely as possible and avoid backing under from the side.

6. Hook up brake hoses and light cords.

7. Make a visual inspection of the fifth wheel jaws to make sure they have closed completely around trailer kingpin.

8. Check to see that the coupler release lever is in the locked position.

9. Be sure the trailer brake system is charged. Then set the trailer brakes with the hand valve or tractor protection valve. Pull against trailer as an additional check that the hookup was successful. Don't pull so hard that you cause damage or undue strain on the equipment.

10. Set the brakes and then raise the landing gear fully before moving coupled unit.

UNHOOKING

1. Line up tractor and trailer in a straight line.

2. Lower the landing gear and block the trailer wheels. Make sure the landing gear is lowered onto solid level ground. Place planks or other levelers under dolly wheels if needed to prevent them from sinking into soft ground.

3. Uncouple brake hoses and light cords and make sure they are clear.

4. Pull coupler release lever to disengage fifth-wheel jaws from trailer kingpin.

5. Pull out from under trailer slowly to permit landing gear to take up the load gradually.

Railroad crossings

Railroad crossings are always dangerous. Every one should be approached with the expectation that a train could be coming. Reduce your speed in accordance with your ability to see any approaching trains in any direction. Speed should be held to a point that will allow you to stop short of the tracks if a stop is necessary. Never rely solely on the pres-

ence of warning signals, gates or flaggers to warn of the approach of a train. Signals might be out of order or a flagger might be lax in the performance of that duty.

Because it is noisy in the cab, don't expect to be able to hear a train horn until the train is dangerously close to the crossing. Because the highway surface at many grade crossings is often rough, crossings must be made at greatly reduced speed to prevent damage to your equipment.

Railroad crossings with steep approaches can cause your unit to "hang up" on the tracks. That danger is greatest when you are using a single-axle tractor to pull a long trailer with the landing gear set back to accommodate a tandem tractor, or when you are pulling a low-slung trailer with limited ground clearance. Failing to negotiate a crossing because of insufficient undercarriage clearance is a disqualification offense.

Never attempt to race a train to a crossing. It is extremely difficult to judge the speed of an approaching train. The train may be coming so fast that you cannot clear the tracks before a collision would occur even though the train may be a long way off when first seen. If you have any doubts, wait for the train to pass.

Never permit traffic conditions to trap you in a position where you have to stop on the railroad tracks. Be sure you can get all the way across the tracks before you start to move. You will be disqualified for 60 days for a first conviction of failing to have enough space to drive through the crossing without stopping.

A full-stop is required at railroad grade crossings whenever:

- The vehicle is transporting hazardous materials required to be marked or placarded, except Divisions 1.5, 1.6, 4.2, 6.2, and Class 9.

- It is a cargo tank vehicle, loaded or empty, that is used to transport hazardous material.

- It is a cargo tank vehicle transporting a material which at the time of loading had a temperature above its flashpoint.

- It is a cargo tank, loaded or empty, transporting a material under a hazardous materials exemption.

- It is a vehicle carrying any amount of chlorine gas.

If a stop is required, it must be made within 50 feet of the crossing, but no closer than 15 feet. Pull as far to the right as possible before stopping and signal to avoid rear-end collisions from following traffic.

Never shift gears while you are crossing railroad tracks.

Double tracks require a double check. Remember that a train on one track may hide a train on the other track. Look both ways before crossing. After one train has cleared a crossing, be sure no other trains are near before starting across the tracks.

Yard areas and grade crossings in cities and towns are just as dangerous as rural grade crossings. Approach them with as much caution.

Clearances

You should be alert to impaired clearances above, on either side, and underneath your equipment. Here are some tips.

Overhead Clearances: Don't rely on posted clearances! Be sure you know the height of your equipment and/or load in order to estimate whether or not there is sufficient clearance for you to pass through the clearance successfully. If over-head clearance is doubtful, stop and check before you proceed.

Overhead clearances can be reduced by accumu-lations of ice and snow, resurfacing of the roadway, uneven road surfaces, flooding, etc. Some tunnels, underpasses, and bridges have adequate clear-ance at the center of the roadway, but not at the edges. So watch out! Such variances are some-times posted, but not always.

Your load also can make a difference in the overall height of the equipment. A unit that clears a low clearance successfully when loaded may hit the overhead clearance when it is empty.

At some underpasses, the grade of the roadway may change. If a downgrade levels off, the vehicle could hit an overhead obstruction well back from the front. But if there is an upgrade, a vehicle may enter safely at one end but strike an overhead obstacle before it emerges from the problem clearance area.

Be sure you have sufficient clearance when driving under an overhead door. If someone is opening and closing the door for your truck, ask them not to let the door move until your truck is clear.

Check for other overhead obstructions like tree limbs, wires, signs, fire escapes, canopies, etc. along the road and on private property.

Side Clearances: Many bridges are narrower than the roadway on either side. Be prepared to yield the right-of-way to oncoming traffic.

When driving on narrow streets or in alleys, watch out for obstacles like signs, street lights, utility poles, parked vehicles, open windows, downspouts, stairways or other obstacles.

Uneven Surfaces: When driving combination units, be sure the landing gear is fully raised to minimize the danger of its striking the ground and becoming damaged and weakened.

When driving a combination vehicle, the greater the distance from the rearmost axle of the tractor to the landing gear, the greater the chance the landing gear has of striking the ground at a sharp change in roadway levels.

When driving equipment with very low ground clearance (e.g., drop-frame or lowbed trailers), avoid places with changes in grade as much as possible to keep from having the unit hang up in a dangerous place, causing damage, and requiring assistance to free it.

Hitting potholes, driving over curbs, or driving over rough surfaces can cause a truck or trailer body to move and strike obstacles on either side, above, or under the unit. Be alert for such places, slow down, and be ready to stop.

Personal safety

Following are some tips on various aspects of personal safety. This section includes information on clothing; lifting and back safety; climbing; door seals and tiedowns; using a hand truck; and fifth wheels and sliding tandems.

Clothing

Always wear clothing that is as neat and clean as the nature of your work permits. On an extended trip you should carry clothing that will allow you to work comfortably outside the vehicle in any kind of weather that could occur along the route. Clothing should be in good condition. Badly worn shoes or ripped and torn clothing can contribute to injuries.

Wear leather gloves when handling freight, opening and closing cargo body doors, or performing other work on or around the unit. Federal regulations require the use of protective footwear where there is a potential for foot injuries.

Follow company dress code or uniform guidelines (if applicable).

Lifting and back safety

When you lift, keep your back straight and use your legs for the actual lifting. Do not hesitate to get help in lifting heavy objects. Get a firm grip on the object being moved. Make sure your hands are not in a position where they can be 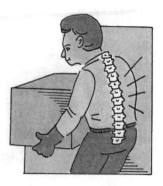 caught between objects. Do not attempt to move objects by grasping steel or plastic banding which can cause severe cuts. Beware of hazards such as wood splinters, protruding nails, loose metal staples, or similar hazards which can cause injury.

When shifting freight from one spot to another, don't twist your body at the waist. Turn your feet and body together in the direction you plan to

move. That way you will protect yourself against
back strain.

Climbing

Be sure of foot and handholds entering and exiting
the cab. Always use a three-point stance — two
feet on the steps and one hand on the handhold;
or two hands on handholds and one foot on the
step. Use the same three-point stance when climbing up or down between the power unit and the
trailer to hook up brake and light lines. Remember
that steps, handholds, gratings, frame rails and
tank tops can be extra slippery with accumulated
oil and moisture.

When you climb into
the trailer body, select
firm foot and hand-
holds. Avoid long
reaches with arms
and legs which put
you off balance or
cause muscle strain. If
handgrips and lad-
ders are installed on
the trailer, use them.
When walking around
your unit at night, use
a flashlight.

Jumping from cabs, trailer bodies, or loading plat-
forms is dangerous and should be avoided. Get
down from an elevated position using the same
means by which you climbed up. Jumping isn't
necessary; in fact it's very risky and can cause
injury.

Door seals and tiedowns

Open trailer doors slowly to avoid being struck by
any falling freight. With swing-back doors, use the
doors as shields against falling freight as you open
each one in turn.

Whenever possible, open and close overhead
doors from the dock to avoid having to climb up
and down on the truck or trailer body. When you
close an overhead door, pull easily at first so the
door will not suddenly come down on you and
cause an injury. When you open or close door
latches, keep your hands clear of pinchpoints
that could result in injury. Wearing sturdy gloves
will help avoid cuts and scrapes from sharp
edges and pinchpoints.

On flatbed equipment, never stand on any part of
the load when applying or releasing tie-downs.
When releasing tie-downs be alert for any shifting of
the load. Be sure you have a clear path of travel to
get out of the way of any freight that may fall off the
vehicle. Also, be careful of the recoil of securement
equipment and doors that may be under pressure.

To remove seals safely, use pliers or wire cutters.

Using a handtruck

When you load a handtruck be sure that the blade is completely under the freight. Place one foot on a wheel to prevent rolling. Grip the far edge of the load and tip both load and the handtruck backward until the weight is balanced directly over the axle. If the freight is too high for you to balance it easily, find some other way to move it. When you're wheeling the truck, watch for objects, cracks or holes that can catch the wheels and trip you and the truck. When you unload, set the freight down gently.

Don't pull handtrucks, push them. If you pull and
the handgrip strikes the back of your leg, it could
cause you to fall, and both handtruck and load will
come down on top of you.

Fifth wheels and sliding tandems

Avoid injury when releasing the fifth wheel to
unhook the trailer, when moving a sliding fifth
wheel, or when moving a sliding tandem. Basic
precautions for heavy lifting are applicable to these
operations to help you avoid strain.

When you unlatch a fifth wheel, be sure you have a
good grip on the release lever. Don't jerk the lever.
Leather gloves will give you a good grip.

It is sometimes necessary to "rock" the unit, in other words move it back and forth, to release the fifth wheel or the locking mechanism on a sliding fifth wheel or the sliding tandem. To avoid injury in this kind of situation, both the driver and the person operating the mechanism must use great care and cooperation. In all cases, you should be ready to stop as soon as the mechanism comes free.

The operator of the release mechanism must keep feet, hands and body as much in the clear as possible and be ready to move away if it releases suddenly. A "pin-puller" is helpful.

When sliding a trailer tandem, the wheels nearest the releasing mechanism should be blocked. If the wheels are pulled over the blocks, there will be an additional warning and more time for the mechanism operator to get clear. Extra care should be exercised if the person operating the mechanism needs to stay under the trailer during the operation.

Notes

Driver security

Security has always been a concern for the transportation industry. But that concern was magnified after the terrorist attacks of September 11, 2001. The world has never been the same since 9-11, and that includes the world of the professional driver. But even with the most high-tech security innovations that your carrier can invest in, you, the driver, are still the most vital link in the supply chain.

The point of origin

Load security begins with all concerned parties knowing exactly who is picking up a given load. When you pick up a load, the shipper may want to verify your identity (photo ID), carrier-assigned vehicle (tractor or truck) number, and carrier-assigned trailer number (if applicable).

After the shipper is satisfied of your identity, the loading process can begin. This is where you step in:

- Do not accept or allow any unauthorized or unscheduled cargo (regardless of size) from being loaded on or in your trailers. This is prohibited.

- Make sure that the right quantity of the right product is put on the trailer.

- Ensure cargo that shows any sign of damage or leakage is not loaded.

- Load the most valuable cargo in the nose of the trailer and as far away from the doors as possible.

- All load-related documentation should be thoroughly reviewed and verified.

- Discrepancies need to be reported and resolved before the paperwork is signed or the trailer is sealed.

- Only sign the bill of lading when you are satisfied that everything is in order.

Once the cargo is signed for and trailer doors are closed and sealed, it becomes you and your carrier's responsibility.

Leaving the shipper

The vast majority of cargo thefts and hijackings occur within a few miles of the load's point of origin. Be especially alert when leaving your shipper. Before leaving:

- Secure the trailer doors with a heavy-duty padlock and/or trailer door seal.

- Keep tractor doors locked and windows rolled up until out on a major road or highway.

- Keep a watchful eye out. If you suspect you are being followed, contact your carrier or the authorities immediately — either from your vehicle or a safe, well-lit, and populated public place such as a reputable truck stop or rest area.

- Be especially alert near signal-regulated highway on and off-ramps. These are prime vehicle hijack areas.

In-transit security

Professional drivers represent the most important factor in any motor carrier's security and theft prevention program. Today's transportation environment requires a heightened sense of awareness and alertness. And, today's drivers must understand that being unaware and inattentive — being careless — are no longer options. While en route, you should:

- Maintain regular communication with your carrier according to their call-in policies.

- Never discuss load-related information. Be very suspicious of anyone asking about your load or destination. Criminals can listen to citizens' band (CB) radios too, so you need to be extremely careful of what you say on the air.

- Stop and park safely and securely. Stop only at reputable truck stops or high-traffic rest areas. Park in well-lit areas where other trucks are present. And of course, always lock the vehicle.

- Be suspicious of anyone asking you to stop. A frequent ploy used by hijackers is to create a scenario which forces or compels the driver to stop.

- Inspect the vehicle. The equipment should be inspected after each stop or rest period. In addition to conducting a normal inspection of safety-related items, you should also check seals and look for anything unusual or suspicious on the vehicle.

- Prepare and execute a well-thought-out trip plan. Drivers hauling hazardous materials — especially hazard classes 1, 2.1, 2.3, 5.2, 6, and 7, or other potentially high-target loads — must route themselves to avoid heavily populated areas. In addition, you should, whenever possible, drive directly to your destination without stopping, or at least trip plan to minimize stops and breaks. A moving target is often the most difficult to hit.

Responding to danger

Use the following tips to avoid danger and potential
injury if you should encounter a cargo theft in
progress:

- Always assume a criminal is armed and
  dangerous.

- Don't be a hero! If you encounter a cargo theft
  in progress or someone trying to break into
  your truck or trailer, call the police or other
  authorities for help immediately.

- If you cannot avoid a hijacking, always do as
  instructed. But also be a good witness. Pay
  attention and listen carefully. After the crime,
  you may be able to provide law enforcement
  with vital information with regard to the
  thieves' methods and where they may have
  taken the vehicle and cargo.

Final destination

Load security ends with the driver and the responsible receiving personnel working together to
unload the trailer.

The driver and receiver should:

- Match bill of lading and/or other load-related
  numbers and paperwork;

- Inspect the seal(s), and match seal number(s) with corresponding documentation;

- Break the seal(s);

- Begin and complete unloading; and

- Sign the bill of lading or other load-related paperwork when they agree on quantity and condition of the cargo.

Notes

Roadside inspections

As the driver of a commercial truck, you will undoubtedly be going through roadside inspections. The main purpose of a roadside inspection is to give you and your vehicle an on-the-spot safety check-up.

A roadside inspection can occur practically anywhere. With advances in technology and enforcement procedures, roadside inspections are no longer limited to being conducted at permanent facilities located along our highways. Portable and mobile inspection sites that can be set up at rest areas, truckstops, or rural roadways are commonplace in many states.

Roadside inspections are referenced in the Federal Motor Carrier Safety Regulations (FMCSR). Section 395.13 addresses out-of-service conditions for drivers and Section 396.9 describes vehicle inspections and what carriers must do to follow up.

Six levels of roadside inspection

The most common and most comprehensive inspection is the Level I inspection, which is a detailed inspection of the vehicle and the driver. The other levels of inspection are components of the Level I inspection or, as with a Level IV inspection, have a very specific focus or purpose (such as a "brakes only" inspection), and are conducted on a very limited basis.

Following are the different levels of inspection:

- **Level I — North American Standard Inspection,** includes examination of documents the driver is required to carry and a detailed vehicle inspection. A Level I inspection takes about 45-60 minutes to complete.

- **Level II — Walk-Around Driver/Vehicle Inspection,** is very similar to the Level I inspection, except the inspector will not check items that require the inspector to physically get under the vehicle. The Level II inspection takes about 30 minutes to complete.

- **Level III — Driver/Credential Inspection,** is an examination of only those documents pertaining to the driver and hazardous materials (if applicable). Your driver's license, medical certificate, logbook and hours of service, and documentation of the annual inspection will be examined. The inspector will also check for the presence of hazardous materials.

- **Level IV — Special Inspection,** usually a one-time examination of a particular item. These examinations are normally made in support of a study or to verify or refute a suspected trend.

- **Level V — Vehicle-Only Inspection,** follows the vehicle portion of the Level I inspection, and may take place without a driver present.

It is usually conducted at a carrier's place of business during a compliance review. It includes all the vehicle components inspected under the Level I inspection.

• **Level VI — Enhanced NAS Inspection for Radioactive Shipments,** is a higher inspection standard than the regular Level I North American Standard Inspection. It is used only on select shipments of radioactive material.

What to expect during a roadside inspection

Remember, the purpose of a roadside inspection is to give you and your vehicle an on-the-spot safety check-up. Think of a roadside inspection as a necessary inconvenience for the sake of everyone's safety, and not as an adversarial relationship between you and the DOT.

Generally, you will be greeted and prepared for the inspection. The inspector will identify himself/herself, and explain the inspection level procedure, chock the vehicle, and ask you to turn off the engine.

Your documents may be examined, including driver's license, medical certificate, driver's log and hours of service, and proof of the annual inspection. The inspector will check for seat belt usage, check the cab for possible illegal presence of alcohol, drugs, weapons, or other contraband, and observe your general appearance as well as your vehicle's overall condition. Your vehicle may or may not be inspected, depending on the level of inspection that is being conducted.

Results of a roadside inspection

At the conclusion of your roadside inspection, the inspector will provide you with an **inspection report** and will explain the violations and defects (if any) that were found as a result of the inspection.

You are required to turn in this form to your company upon arrival at the next terminal or facility. If you're not going to be at a company facility within the next 24 hours, you must mail it to your company.

In general, there are three possible outcomes of a roadside inspection:

1. If no violations were found, you will be free to go on your way. The inspection report must still be forwarded to your company as described above.

2. If one or more violations were found, but you were not placed out of service, you will be allowed to go on your way. However, within 15 days of the inspection, your company must correct any violations or defects noted on the inspection form, sign it, and return it to the issuing agency.

3. If one or more violations or defects were found that are so unsafe that they must be corrected before operations can resume, you and/or your vehicle will be placed out of service. The inspector will inform you what needs to be done or corrected before you can drive again.

CVSA inspection decal

A vehicle (bus, truck, truck tractor, semitrailer, or trailer) that passes a Level I or Level V inspection will be awarded a decal. "Pass Inspection" means that no violations were found.

Decals apply to the vehicle only. The decal will be affixed to the vehicle by the certified inspector. Decals remain valid for no longer than three months. Generally, vehicles displaying a valid decal are not subject to re-inspection unless a problem is observed.

What is the surest way to pass a roadside inspection and not be placed out of service? *Be in compliance with the regulations!* It is as simple as that.

Notes

Fire prevention

Here are some tips to remember on fire prevention. Most are common sense, but can serve as good reminders for you.

Turn off the engine when you are refueling. Don't smoke or allow any other open ignition source within 50 feet of your unit.

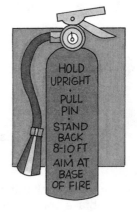

HOLD
UPRIGHT
·
PULL
PIN
·
STAND
BACK
8-10 FT
·
AIM AT
BASE
OF FIRE

Don't use gasoline for cleaning clothes or any part of your equipment. Use only an approved solvent.

Don't let refuse, matchbooks, papers, oily rags and the like accumulate in the cab of your tractor. Good housekeeping can help prevent fires.

If you are carrying fusees, they should be kept in their holders to avoid friction fires. Lighted fusees should not be attached to any part of a vehicle.

If you smoke, use extreme care. Make sure matches, cigarettes, cigars and pipe ashes are out and completely cool before throwing them away.

Make sure drafts from open cab windows don't blow ashes where they can start fires.

Smoking is completely prohibited when you are transporting hazardous materials or when you are moving freight of any type into or out of the vehicle's cargo area.

Tire fires are much easier to prevent than to put out.

   a.   Check tires at all safety stops and change any tire that is soft or flat.

   b.   NEVER run for any distance on a soft or flat tire.

   c.   Do not use your truck after a hot tire has been discovered until you either remove it or wait until it is cool enough to touch. Never place a hot tire in the spare tire rack without giving it a chance to cool.

Never drive a unit with the parking brake or any wheel brake unreleased. Heat builds up quickly under such conditions and can easily start a fire.

Fire fighting

Don't ever take chances in fighting a fire that will endanger your personal safety. Truck fires call for quick thinking and planning to get the best results from the limited equipment at hand. Fire extinguishers required on trucks will be exhausted in

8-10 seconds. Plan where and how to use the amount of extinguisher agent that you have available to its best advantage. A minute lost in inspection and planning will not lose the truck, but waste of extinguishing agent may.

If there is a water supply nearby that can be reached without parking where vehicles or buildings are endangered, get to it and ask for help, if possible. If a fire department is nearby, contact them to solicit their aid as quickly as you can. Literally every second counts. Do not use water on an oil fire. Water only spreads an oil fire.

When using your fire extinguisher, try to fight the fire with the wind at your back so you don't have to inhale the smoke and fumes from the extinguisher. If you are fighting an engine fire, open the hood as little as possible. And if you have an electrical fire, disconnect the battery as quickly as you can.

Above all, try to stretch the contents of your fire extinguisher. Use only enough extinguishing agent at a time to knock down the flames. Save the rest for possible future use.

Fire extinguishers usually carried on a truck WILL NOT put out a tire fire. If you can get help from a fire department or get to a source of water, do so. If you can remove the tire without endangering yourself or anybody who is assisting you, do so. Shoveling dirt on a burning tire will sometimes control the fire until you can remove the wheel.

A cargo fire in a closed van will usually be discovered when you smell smoke or notice smoke escaping around the doors. Such a fire can only smolder because of lack of oxygen as long as you keep the doors closed. **DO NOT ALLOW ANYONE TO OPEN THE DOORS** until the unit is parked in a safe location and help is available; preferably from a fire department. Then open the doors cautiously, but be prepared for a flare-up. If it's safe to do so, remove any undamaged cargo in order to reach the fire. To prevent unnecessary cargo damage, don't use water until the source of the fire is reached.

In the case of any fire, use your best possible judgment under the circumstances. If a fire does get out of control despite your attempts to fight it, you may need to unhook the power unit from a burning trailer and save the tractor.

Notes

Handling some special situations

You should always comply with posted road warnings and highway notices. These signs are there for your protection and information. Keep the following things in mind as you move along:

- A group of people on or near the road could indicate potential trouble. Slow down, keep your road position, and be ready to stop or take other appropriate action.

- Animals on or near the road are also a clear warning to keep your vehicle under good control. Pay attention to signs warning of various animal hazards, from deer crossings to cattle crossings, etc. If you do encounter animals in the road unexpectedly, try to make a straight stop. Attempting to swerve is likely to result in an overturn. You cannot rely on fences to keep livestock out of the road.

- Be alert for unexpected changes in traffic flow. Slowdowns can occur on any road at any time. Adjust your speed promptly to changing conditions. Don't get into a situation where a sudden lane change would be your last hope of avoiding an accident.

- In the event of a sudden front tire failure, concentrate on steering to keep control of the vehicle. Full-throttle acceleration can help stabilize the front end, but then back off the accelerator and let the unit slow down. Don't use the brakes because that will only cause the vehicle to turn more sharply in the direction of the failed tire. Be alert for a change in ride or handling that could indicate a tire failure at some other wheel position.

- If one of your wheels runs off the pavement, concentrate on steering. Hard braking or a sudden swerve is likely to result in loss of control or even an overturn. Keep going straight and let the unit lose speed gradually. When your speed is substantially reduced, steer back onto the pavement at a sharp angle and then countersteer to keep from going into the lane of opposing traffic or going across and off the pavement on the other side of the highway.

Controlling speed and noise

Always comply with posted speed limits in urban and residential areas and when going through small towns.

Try to minimize noise produced by your CMV by operating with a light throttle and avoiding high engine speed in urbanized areas. Avoid using your air horns and engine retarders (jake brakes) in built-up areas. Be alert for signs prohibiting or limiting use of engine brakes in urbanized areas and obey the local rulings — it's all part of being a good neighbor.

Slow down in school zones; remember that children cannot be expected to exercise good judgment in traffic all of the time.

Adverse driving conditions

Reduce speed when visibility and traction are reduced by rain, fog, snow, ice, or similar conditions. Never assume that conditions of reduced visibility and traction will be of short duration. Keep your speed down until you know for sure that you are in the clear.

Most skids result from sudden stops and turns on slippery pavement. Drive carefully and try to antici-pate emergencies so that you can avoid last-minute maneuvers that may mean loss of control.

Avoid wheel lock-up when stopping on slippery pavement. When fanning your brakes, don't let the air pressure drop below 60 pounds. And drivers operating vehicles that are equipped with antilock braking systems (ABS) should remember that these brakes won't help avoid accidents unless you adjust your speed to existing road conditions. ABS is designed to help you maintain control by avoiding the problem of wheel lockup. But it does not reduce overall stopping distances.

When operating a combination unit you must remember that not all elements in the combination will necessarily be equipped with ABS. That means you will also need to be able to modulate the brakes when driving a unit not equipped with ABS. You must be prepared to release the brakes, and start fanning, if any non-ABS equipped vehicle in the combination begins to slide out of control.

If conditions become too hazardous, it is best to stop in a safe place. Then advise your company of the delay and its expected duration. These days with many drivers having cell phones, close contact with your carrier is simplified considerably. If you must leave the unit for some reason, be sure to leave a note saying where you have gone.

Exercise extreme care if you encounter a flooded area as you travel. Check with those controlling traffic in the problem area before crossing and follow their directions to the letter.

Reduce your speed and maintain close control when strong winds are blowing. Pay attention to any signs warning of unsafe wind conditions. Problems with winds are especially likely to occur if you are driving empty equipment on slippery roads.

Construction zones

Road maintenance and construction always present potential hazards. Your best defense in these areas is to slow down and be alert for traffic back-ups. Always be sure you can stop safely.

If lanes are closed, maneuver yourself into the specified lane well in advance. Don't drive next to another truck to deliberately block automobile traffic.

Watch for maintenance/construction personnel and equipment. Pay attention to the directions of flaggers. Always be ready to stop safely. In unpaved areas, drive slowly to minimize dust and wear and tear on the equipment.

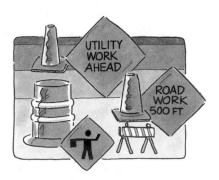

Descending grades

Gravity's pull forces all vehicles to speed up on downgrades. To help combat the forces of gravity when traveling downhill, select:

- An appropriate speed;

- A low gear; and

- Proper braking technique.

An appropriate speed is one that is slow enough to allow a vehicle's brakes to hold the vehicle without the brakes overheating and fading. If you have to continually increase the pressure applied to the brakes to get the same stopping power, the brakes will eventually fade until there's little to no stopping control. When selecting an appropriate speed, consider:

- The total weight of the vehicle and its cargo;

- The grade's steepness and length; and

- Weather and road conditions.

The braking effect of the engine should be used as the primary way to control the vehicle's speed. The engine's braking effect is greatest when it is near the governed RPMs and the transmission is in the lower gears.

Before starting down a grade, shift the transmission into a low gear. Once a vehicle's speed has been built up it will be difficult, if not impossible, to downshift. Attempting to downshift can cause the vehicle to lose all braking effect, creating a dangerous situation.

How brakes can fail — Any time a brake is used, heat is created. The rubbing of the brake pad against the brake drum or disc is what creates this heat. Excessive heat, caused by excessive braking can cause brakes to fail.

All brakes must be adjusted and operating properly to safely and efficiently control a vehicle. If some brakes are out of adjustment, others may become overworked, causing them to overheat and fade, leaving a driver with little or no braking control.

As with all vehicle components, brake adjustment should be checked often, but it should be given even more attention when you are ready to head downhill.

Braking technique — The following is proper braking technique for a vehicle traveling in the proper, low gear.

1. Identify a safe speed for the load and grade.

2. When that speed is reached, apply the brakes hard enough to feel a definite slowdown.

3. Once the vehicle's speed has been reduced by 5 mph below the vehicle's safe speed, release the brakes. The application of the brakes should last about 3 seconds.

4. When the vehicle's speed increases back to or above the safe speed, repeat the first two steps.

For example, if the vehicle's safe speed is 30 mph; don't apply the brakes until the vehicle's speed has reached 30 mph. Then the brakes should be applied just hard enough to gradually reduce the vehicle's speed to 25 mph. Once at 25 mph, the brakes may be released.

Ascending grades

You are really fighting gravity when you ask your rig to ascend a steep grade. Gravity adds to your load weight and makes it that much harder to make it up the grade successfully and safely. More horsepower is required just to keep moving.

You will probably have to gear down as you ascend a fairly steep grade. The key is to shift before your engine rpm get too low — try to find a gear that will give you sufficient rpm as you move up the slope. Keep a close eye on your dashboard indicators as you climb — overheating can easily result.

Finally, upgrades are NOT the time to think about passing! You just won't be able to do it efficiently, so patience is the key.

Mirrors

Making effective use of the mirrors you have available is extremely important. It's especially crucial that you check the mirrors before you change either speed or your position in traffic — that will prevent any unfortunate surprises.

A good rule of thumb is to check your mirrors approximately every four seconds. Be especially aware of potential blind spots beside the tractor's fuel tank and drive wheels. CMVs generally come equipped with two types of mirrors — plane and convex. The plane mirror by itself allows too large a blind spot, and a convex mirror gives a distorted view. Each has specific value, however.

Plane mirrors — A plane mirror provides the best view of the rear of your trailer and the highway behind you. However, it doesn't give a very wide view and has a blind area along most of the length of the vehicle. Field of view is best in the left mirror. Images in the side mirrors are similar to those on an automobile. You should be able to easily learn to judge speed and distance of overtaking vehicles. Because of the blind spots, lane changes and other maneuvers are fairly risky, so be certain that you still use your signals and pause a bit before changing direction.

Convex mirrors — These mirrors are designed with an outward curvature to provide a wide angle view. They give a broader view than plane mirrors do and also eliminate a lot of the blind spot area. In addition, they provide the best close-up view of the side portions of your tractor-trailer combination. The downside of convex mirrors, however, is that they show a distorted image. For example, vehicles overtaking you appear smaller and farther away than they actually are. Small, stick-on convex mirrors that many drivers make use of have the most distortion and also reduce the plane mirror viewing area.

Combination of mirrors best — A good combination of mirrors will provide both maximum side and rear vision. However, a combination takes some getting used to for the driver. The overlapping view can confuse the driver. It will be helpful to have a high-quality, properly aligned and adjusted convex mirror so that overlap and distortion is minimized as much as possible. Be aware that even with a good combination of mirrors, some blind spots will still remain. You should get used to the position and field of view that each of your mirrors provides. Don't ever move your vehicle without checking to be sure that the mirrors are properly positioned.

Mirrors require care from you as a driver. Keep them clean and tight so they have the maximum effectiveness. If mirrors are not tight, they will vibrate and distort the view you have of the traffic situation you find yourself in at any moment. Adjust them to give yourself the very best view possible.

Cell phones

As of 2007, 32 states have, or allow cities within their state to have, a restriction on the use of cell phones by some or all drivers. Also, be sure you are very clear on any company policy that may be in place that prohibits cell phone usage while you are behind the wheel.

Some additional states or municipalities either already have such prohibitions in effect, or are contemplating them. Here are links to two websites that track cell phone legislation; in case you want to do some research on your own:

> http://www.statehighwaysafety.org/html/ stateinfo/laws/cellphone_laws.html - Governors Highway Safety Association;

> http://www.ncsl.org/programs/transportation/ 2006cellphoneup.htm - National Conference of State Legislatures.

If you stop to think about it, it only makes good common sense to stop your vehicle in a safe location before talking on your cell phone. It's just too difficult to concentrate on your job of driving and to pay attention to a telephone conversation. For example, in 2003, the National Transportation Safety Board (NTSB) made the following recommendations as a way to deal with the issue of distracted driving. NTSB recommended to all states — except New Jersey, which already had such a proscription — to prohibit holders of learner's permits and intermediate licenses from using interactive wireless communication devices while driving.

NTSB also urged the National Highway Traffic Safety Administration (NHTSA) to develop a media campaign stressing dangers of distracted driving, and that it should work with the American Driver and Traffic Safety Education Association to develop driver training curricula that emphasize the risks of distracted driving. NTSB cited a study showing that drivers engaged in phone conversations were unaware of traffic movements around them. In addition, NTSB said that NHTSA should determine the magnitude and impact of driver-controlled, in-vehicle distractions, including the use of interactive wireless communication devices, on highway safety and report its findings to the United States Congress and the states.

If you have an accident

The first order of business is to STOP. Failure to stop at the scene of an accident in which you are involved is a criminal offense and will result in disciplinary action in addition to any penalties that may be imposed by the authorities. A conviction of leaving the scene of an accident while driving a commercial vehicle will result in disqualification.

Set out your warning devices, in accordance with DOT safety regulations. If the accident occurs near the crest of a hill or in a curve, set emergency signals farther out, but not more than 500 feet away.

Assist any injured persons, but DON'T move them unless absolutely necessary. Keep them warm and quiet, pending arrival of an ambulance, doctor, or other authorities.

Notify law enforcement. If it's not possible to telephone, write a brief, carefully-worded note and ask another motorist to phone or give it to the police. LEAVE YOUR VEHICLE UNATTENDED ONLY IN EXTREME EMERGENCY.

In case of serious accident and in EVERY case where a fatality or personal injury occurs, be sure that your nearest company terminal or agent is notified so that the insurance company can be contacted without delay. If no company official can be reached, notify the nearest office of the insurance carrier that's listed in your accident report kit, and ask them to contact the proper company official.

Fill out a preliminary accident report card. Be sure to get names of all witnesses BOTH FOR AND AGAINST YOU. If witnesses refuse to give their names, get the license number of their vehicles. Regardless of facts, ADMIT NOTHING, PROMISE NOTHING, and DON'T ARGUE. Be polite. Give your name, the company name, and offer to show your driver's license.

Take pictures, if possible (many accident kits include a camera to document accidents). Don't move or allow to be moved any vehicles involved until someone arrives who can verify or witness the position of vehicles, length and position of skid marks, etc. Never obliterate the company name on your vehicle at an accident scene.

Stay at the location of the accident until you are instructed by law enforcement, and a company or insurance company representative to proceed.

You should, without fail, report EVERY accident you have even though very minor. Failure to report any accident can subject you to disciplinary action.

In case of serious accidents, where personal injury is involved or there is a large amount of property damage, you could be suspended from work while the accident is under investigation.

When you report an accident by phone or messenger; be specific on location, time, extent of injury or damage, condition of cargo, and where you can be reached. If you call a terminal, be sure you talk to someone authorized to act on a report. Make a note of that person's name for the future.

The information needed on every accident includes the following:

a.   Date, time, exact location.

b.   For every involved vehicle: make, model, type, license number, insurance company, owner's name and address.

c.   Names and addresses of drivers and passengers in each involved vehicle and the vehicle occupied by each person.

d.   Name and address of each injured person, extent of injuries, where hospitalized.

e.   Names and addresses of owners of all other damaged property.

f.   Descriptions and estimates of all damage to vehicles and property.

g. Names and addresses of witnesses, license numbers of first vehicles on scene, and nearby addresses where witnesses might be found.

h. Names, badge numbers, and departments of investigating police officers.

Try to make as accurate a diagram of the accident scene as you can, which should clearly indicate:

a. Terrain — is there an upgrade, downgrade, or is it level?

b. Are there any obstructions to view, buildings, trees, parked vehicles, etc?

c. What are the location and type of traffic signs and signals?

d. What was the path of travel of involved vehicles before impact, at the point of impact, and after impact? Show yours as Vehicle 1.

e. Type of road — Is it 2-lane, 4-lane, divided, etc.?

Get important measurements such as road and lane width, sight distances, distances from fixed landmarks, etc. by pacing or measuring. Allow $2\frac{1}{2}$ feet per pace.

Notes

Taking care of yourself on the road

Your job as a professional driver is a stressful one. When you are behind the wheel, you must be constantly alert, and you are also under pressure to pick up and deliver loads — no matter what the circumstances may be. Add to that the loneliness involved in being away from family and friends a good deal of the time (if you are an over-the-road driver), and you have a recipe for trouble. Your best defense against all of these factors is to take superior care of yourself on the road. If you're not nice to yourself, who's going to be? In this section you will find some tips and suggestions on how you can take good care of yourself on the road. It will include eating right and physical and mental exercise tips.

Eating right is a big factor

Eating right when you are away from home isn't easy. Blessedly, it is getting easier to find good healthy food at truck stops. But if you have any kind of chronic health problem to deal with — high blood pressure, high cholesterol, diabetes, etc., you have a special challenge to stay on your diet while you are on the road.

What is a healthy diet? You have probably been hearing about those basic food groups since you were a kid. But do you really have a good idea of what foods fall into the basic nutritional categories? Be aware that the categories and structure changed somewhat in early 2005, but the nutritional principles of balance and variety remain the same. Knowing what you have to work with helps in planning a good, healthy diet at home or on the road. So, let's take a look at some food groups.

Meat group choices — This group will be the prime source of protein in your diet. Included are beef and pork, all poultry, fish and shellfish, lamb and veal, in addition to variety meats (liver, heart, kidney). Eggs are also a choice in this group, along with non-meat items that are good protein sources (dry beans, peas and lentils; nuts of all kinds; peanut butter). **How much?** Two or more servings from this group each day are recommended. A serving is considered to be 3 ounces of meat (without bones), one egg, 2 tablespoons of peanut butter, 1 cup of beans/peas/lentils.

Vegetable-fruit group choices — Foods included in this group are self-explanatory. These foods are primary suppliers of Vitamins C and A in your diet. **C sources:** Oranges and grapefruit and their juices; cantaloupe, strawberries, and some exotic fruits (mango, papaya, guava); broccoli, Brussels sprouts, green and sweet red peppers are all good C sources. Fair sources include honeydew and watermelon, lemons and tangerines and their juices, tomatoes or tomato juice, asparagus, potatoes and sweet potatoes (in their jackets), spinach and greens (collards, kale, mustard, turnip), raw cabbage, kohlrabi. **A sources:** dark green and deep yellow vegetables (broccoli, chard, collards, cress, kale, spinach, turnip greens, carrots, pumpkin, sweet potatoes, winter squash), along with some fruits like apricots, cantaloupes, mangoes, persimmons. **How much?** Four or more servings from this group each day are recommended. A serving is considered to be ½ cup of the vegetable or fruit chosen, or a regular portion (one orange, one potato, half a grapefruit, etc.)

Milk group choices — This group is a major source of Vitamin D in your diet. Besides milk in all forms, this group includes cottage and cream cheese, as well as all types of cheeses, ice cream and yogurt. **How much?** Adults should have the equivalent of 2 8-ounce glasses of milk per day. Some serving substitutions follow:

$^1/_2$ cup of yogurt = $^1/_2$ glass milk
1-inch cube of cheese = $^1/_2$ glass milk
$^1/_2$ cup cottage cheese = $^1/_3$ glass milk.

Nutrition experts recommend that at least part of the daily requirement be consumed in the form of milk itself.

Bread-cereal group choices — Besides being a good source of vitamins and minerals, this group is a major source of fiber and energy-producing carbohydrates in your diet. Foods included are wholegrain or enriched breads and cereals in all their variety — cooked and ready-to-eat cereals, cornmeal and grits, all pasta products, bulgur and rice, crackers, quick breads and any baked goods made with enriched flour. **How much?** Four or more servings from this group each day are recommended. One serving might be a slice of bread, an ounce of ready-to-eat cereal or ¾ cup of cooked cereal, pasta, rice, etc.

Other food choices — To help round out your meals, and add flavor and energy, you will want to eat some fats (butter, margarine, etc.) and some sugars. **How much?** Just be aware of the need for a well-balanced diet. A little goes a long way when it comes to refined sugar and fat, but your body does need some fat, etc. Just don't get carried away.

Check your fitness level

As a trucker you sit for long hours, and do a job that doesn't give you much opportunity for physical exercise. One way to help counteract these bad situations is to move around a little whenever you get out of the cab. If part of your job is unloading the truck, you know what it's like to go from sitting for a couple of hours (or longer) to lifting and moving cargo. You get plenty of exercise then — probably the equivalent of a workout at a gym. But the person at the gym has probably stretched out those muscles before beginning the real workout. Have you?

Muscles work most efficiently when they are warmer than normal body temperature. That's the reason dancers and body builders warm up before beginning their real workout. You can easily injure yourself if you don't take time to do that.

A simple warm-up sequence — After you get out of the cab, take just a few minutes to reach your arms well over your head to one side and stretch as high as you can. Then reach over your head to the opposite side. Bend from your waist forward (as far as you can to stretch the back), backward, and from side to side.

Put one foot on the cab step, with the other one on the ground. Push into the bent leg, giving a good long stretch to the extended leg. Repeat the process with the other leg. Keep your movements slow and easy.

An easy on-the-road workout — Why not give some thought to including some weights and/or a spring exerciser in your gear when you are on the road. And watch for fitness centers, etc. that are accessible to truckers. Meantime, some barbells, an exercise mat and a simple training record to let you keep track of your efforts will get your started. You can even do some simple things right behind the wheel.

Moderate physical activity is also good for your mental state. Exercise, even for a short time, reduces depression and anxiety as well as fatigue. And, as another bonus, it helps you manage any stress you may be feeling.

Exercising while on the road — When you are away from home, keep your eyes open for exercise possibilities that you can get to with your truck. And become creative in designing some simple programs for yourself that will improve your personal fitness. One easy one is to park as far away from the truck stop buildings as you can, and use the walk as part of your exercise program.

Fitness off the road — And when you are at home, don't just "crash" at the end of the day because you don't feel like exercising. That's a good time to do it — your body can still get going when your mind is tired. You may be surprised that you feel better after a short workout. The best time to <u>read</u> is after your body is relaxed after exercise.

Deal effectively with emotions

Emotions are part of life. You can feel excited and "up" one day and then sad or depressed the next day. How you feel only becomes a problem when your emotions begin to affect your performance.

Anger is the mental state that causes the most problems. Imagine a really angry driver, and you are looking at a case of "road rage" just waiting to happen. Such a person is uptight, has a rapid heartbeat and breathing, and slowed digestion. The body is prepared for a fight. This "ready" condi-

tion results in erratic braking, steering, and acceleration behaviors.

Usually emotions tend to abate with the passage of time. But if you remain angry for an extended period of time, you will also become physically tired. Mentally, an angry driver also has trouble making reasoned decisions. And he/she may not see things that are ahead.

Some coping techniques to try — Since your total concentration needs to be on driving when you are behind that wheel, you need to learn to cope with your emotions. Try these methods:

- **Practice safe, consistent, and dependable driving habits** — if you have good habits, they will see you through temporary periods of high stress,

- **Mentally prepare yourself to meet stressful conditions** — that one-lane construction zone around the bend or the speeder who is coming up fast in your rearview mirror will bother you less if you know you can handle it,

- **Know your own reactions and be honest about them** — if you have a temper, accept that as part of your personality and take steps to see if you can lengthen your "fuse" a bit,

- **Be aware that stress and emotions often surface when your body is tired** — get enough rest and practice releasing tension.

Try these relaxation techniques — To get rid of emotional stress and tension, here are some simple relaxation techniques to try:

- **Stop the truck if you can, get out and stretch; then exercise briefly.** A little physical exertion improves your mental attitude. Simple exercises work just fine.

- **If you can't stop at all, try breathing deeply and regularly while you are going down the road.** Practice letting tension out of your body as you exhale.

- **Listen to music** and concentrate only on your driving in order to turn your mind away from the cause of the tension.

- **Accept the things you cannot change.** Talk about what's on your mind with someone you can trust so problems don't keep building up inside you.

Care and operation of equipment

Professional drivers do not abuse their equipment. They take real pride in the units they drive and in their ability to drive them properly, and to care for them. They recognize the importance of getting small problems taken care of promptly before they become big problems. The more you know about how your equipment should function, the more you can contribute to longer equipment life and lower operating costs.

Remember to check all instruments regularly while you are driving. They are often the first warning of problems.

Don't drive over curbing or other obstructions. Be sure to reduce your speed when you drive on rough roads. When you brake for an obstruction, release the brakes to let the wheels roll free before actually striking the object. Avoid driving over glass or rocks on the highway to minimize tire damage. Watch clearances overhead, on each side and under-neath to avoid needless damage.

INSPECTION OF EQUIPMENT: Company rules and DOT regulations require that you be satisfied that your vehicle is in safe operating condition at the start of each day's driving. The driver must review and sign the review copy of the vehicle condition report prepared by the previous driver. The step-by-step walkaround procedure given below will assist you in determining whether the vehicle is in safe operating condition.

1. As you approach the vehicle note its general condition. Look for leakage of water, fuel or lubricants under vehicle.

2. In the engine compartment check water and crankcase levels. Check the fan and compressor belts for cracks and excessive slack and wear. Note the general condition of the engine space.

3. Start the engine and set it at a fast idle for warm-up. Check for abnormal engine noise. Check gauges for normal readings. The low air pressure warning should operate if air pressure is below 60 pounds. The antilock warning light should light briefly and then go out (on vehicles with anti-lock brakes).

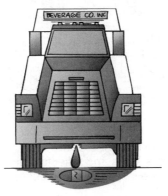

4. Check the emergency equipment, horn(s), windshield wipers. Turn on all lights including 4-way flasher switch for turn signals. Check the steering wheel free-play.

5. Leave the cab to check headlights and turn signals. Switch headlight beams and check, then turn off headlights only, but leave other lights on.

6. Check the front clearance and identification lights.

7. Check the left and right front wheels, tires, lugs, studs. Check for grease leaks around hubs.

8. Check the right side of cab, door, mirrors, etc. and check lights and reflectors along the right side as the inspection progresses.

9. Check the right rear tractor tires, wheels, lugs or studs. Note any leaking grease or oil.

10. Check the trailer light and brake lines for secure connections. Be sure manual shutoff valves are open. Be sure the lines are properly secured to prevent entangling or chafing.

11. Check the hookup: fifth wheel, jaws, release lever on tractor-trailer; pintle-hook, tow-bar, safety chains, and converter gear on full-trailer unit.

12. Check the right trailer tires, wheels, lugs or studs. Check for any thrown lubricant.

13. Check the rear of the body, mudflaps, rear lights (clearance and identification, stop, tail, turn signals), rear reflectors, rear end protection.

14. Check the left trailer tires, wheels, lugs or studs. Check lights and reflectors on left side as the inspection progresses.

15. Check left rear tractor tires, wheels, lugs or studs. Check for any thrown lubricant.

16. Re-enter the cab. Re-check all the gauges. Air pressure should be at maximum.

17. Check the parking brake.

18. Check the brakes and stoplights. With a fully charged system, check the air brakes as follows:

   a. Apply parking brakes (usually by pulling the yellow parking brake control valve). All brakes equipped with spring-brake chambers should apply. Air-applied parking brakes should apply as well as the brakes on trailers that are not equipped with spring-brakes.

   b. Release the parking brakes.

   c. Push in the red octagonal trailer air supply control knob if it automatically popped out when you applied the parking brake.

d.   Use treadle (foot) valve to apply and release brakes to check for proper action.

e.   Turn off the engine. Rapidly apply and release the treadle valve to fan down the air pressure. The low air pressure warning should operate before either air pressure gauge needle shows less than 60 psi. The red octagonal knob* which controls the tractor protection valve should pop out and apply trailer brakes when the highest needle pressure reads between 45 and 20 psi.

f.   Recharge the air system to 100-120 psi then check for leaks:

o   Release the parking brakes and apply service brakes with engine off. After 5 seconds, there should be no audible leaks or further pressure drop.

o   If there is a pressure drop, or audible air leaks are noticed, the condition must be repaired before driving.

*On older trucks using flipper valves instead of red octagonal knobs, disconnect the control (service) gladhand and make a steady light brake application. Pressure should stabilize between 20 and 45 psi.

19. Turn off the 4-way flasher and activate the left and right turn signals. Proper operation of turn signals can be ascertained by checking the operation of the front ones.

20. If you are transporting hazardous materials, be sure that any required placards on front, rear and both sides are correct and read the same. Check the shipping papers.

21. Fasten your seatbelt.

22. Make a test stop before leaving yard. Drain air tanks daily, unless equipped with spitter valve. Check tires at the start of the trip and each time you park the vehicle. See §397.17

Any defects found during your pretrip inspection should be reported to the shop and corrected before departure.

REQUIRED ENROUTE INSPECTION: Stop and recheck your equipment periodically during each trip or tour of duty:

1. At least every 3 hours or 150 miles, whichever comes first.

2. Stop to check the lights before dark, and recheck them at every night stop.

3. Federal regulations require the following enroute checks:

    a. Hazardous Materials — Tires must be checked at the beginning of each trip and each time the vehicle is parked.

        o   If a tire is underinflated, you can drive the vehicle to the nearest point where the condition can be corrected.

        o   If a hot tire is found, it must be removed, and the vehicle cannot be driven until the condition has been corrected.

    b. Load Condition — Unless the load is sealed or is so loaded that it cannot be checked, it must be checked:

        o   Within the first 50 miles of driving;

        o   At each change of duty status, every 3 hours or 150 miles, whatever occurs first.

DRIVER VEHICLE INSPECTION REPORTS (DVIR): Federal regulations and company rules require a written report of the condition of each unit you have driven:

1. A report must be prepared and submitted at the conclusion of each day's work.

2.   The written report must be prepared and sub-
     mitted even if no defects were detected by the
     driver.

3.   If a trip extends over several days, a DVIR
     must be prepared at least once every 24 hours
     (end of each day's work).

4.   If a condition cannot be adequately written up
     on the DVIR, you can also report it in person to
     your supervisor or the shop, as appropriate.

CARE OF CAB BODY: Check for pre-existing
body damage during your pretrip inspection. At a
company terminal, you can report such damage to
a supervisor before you leave. When you are not at
a company facility, just contact your supervisor and
note the damage on the DVIR. If you don't follow
proper procedure, you could be held responsible
for the damage.

Be sure to clean and adjust mirrors. Clean windshield and windows inside and out. Close cab doors carefully to prevent glass breakage. Clean all lights and reflectors (including reflective tape).

Drive carefully to avoid body damage from striking stationary objects, or being involved in any type of collision. Minor contacts with tree limbs, poles, signs, etc. can cause costly damage.

Be sure the cargo body is secure with doors closed, latched, and sealed, if required.

ENGINE COMPARTMENT: Do not tamper with or make any adjustments to the engine, fuel system or other components. Where required or permitted, know how to check engine oil and coolant levels and how to add fluids if necessary.

When the unit is parked, check underneath for signs of leaking fuel, oil, or coolant. Never remove the cap from an overheated radiator. Let the system cool down. Open the cap to the first notch and let the pressure vent before you remove the cap. Add water with the engine at a fast idle.

If the engine has automatic shut-down devices for low oil pressure or high temperature, you have only 30-45 seconds to find a safe parking place after the initial warning happens.

TIRES AND WHEELS: Tires, wheels, lugs, and studs should be inspected every time a vehicle inspection is done and as part of every enroute safety inspection. A tire pressure gauge is the only accurate way to check tire pressure. Get yourself one. Tires should be gauged when they are cold. Never let air out of a tire under any circumstances.

"Thumping" tires with a hammer or tire club can tell you that the tire has air in it, but not how much. Thumping should be done during an enroute inspection when the tires are warm from running down the road and a gauge would not be accurate. Thumping can locate tires that are severely under-inflated, and in need of immediate repair.

If it is necessary to change one tire of a set of duals, it should be replaced with a tire of matching size. If this isn't possible, always put the larger-diameter tire in the outside position. After a tire has been changed in any position, recheck the lugs within the next 50 miles and retighten them if necessary. If a hydraulic jack is carried, keep it upright. After use, depress plunger and close valve to prevent leakage.

ENGINE/TRANSMISSION CARE: Allow the engine to warm up while you are doing the pretrip inspection. Then, drive at a moderate speed until engine is thoroughly warmed up. This also allows the transmission, other drive-line components, and wheel bearings to warm up gradually.

After a sustained run, allow a diesel engine to idle for 2-4 minutes to cool down, and then shut it off. Do not leave the engine idling when the temperature is above freezing. If a stop will be less than 30 minutes, the engine can be safely shut off even at colder temperatures. Unnecessary idling consumes as much as one gallon of fuel per hour and causes severe wear and tear on the engine. In many places, engine idling is restricted by law as an air pollution control measure.

Always use the gear that will keep your engine speed within the range recommended by the manufacturer. For fuel-efficient driving, don't downshift when the engine speed is above the recommended minimum. Engage the clutch smoothly and shift without clashing the gears. It saves needless wear and tear on your equipment and is the mark of a professional driver.

Finally, be alert to any potential problems that are indicated by gauges or warning lights, or unusual sounds, smells, or vibrations.

SERVICE (FOOT) BRAKES: Except where specifically noted, the information in this section applies to air-brake systems. Regardless of the type of brakes it has, do not operate a vehicle with defective or ineffective brakes beyond the first point at which it can be safely parked.

On a straight truck equipped with hydraulic brakes, a low pedal is an indication of the need for adjustment. If the pedal sinks toward the floor under steady pressure, it indicates a leak which should be repaired without delay.

Check the air pressure gauge(s) frequently. Current vehicles have both a primary and secondary air system. In normal operation, the pressure for both systems should read about the same. If there is a big difference, or the audible/visible low-air warning activates, stop in the nearest safe location until the air loss is corrected. If there is a loss of pressure in the primary system, continued pressure on the treadle valve will activate the secondary system and allow you to make a safe stop.

Don't attempt to adjust the brakes on a unit unless you are qualified and authorized to do so by your company policy, have received necessary instruction, and have the required tools. Never attempt to adjust any type of self-adjusting brakes.

PARKING BRAKES: Know the type of parking brakes on your unit:

  a. A system that acts on the rear wheels like those on a passenger car (only on small straight trucks); or,

  b. A brake on the driveshaft that is activated by a lever; or,

  c. An air-activated system controlled by a diamond-shaped yellow knob with the brakes generally applied by spring pressure (spring-brakes) used on most air-braked vehicles.

Except in an emergency parking brakes should never be applied while a vehicle is moving. To do so may result in wheel lockup and loss of control. It can also seriously damage the parking brake and related sections of the equipment.

When you start out, be sure that all brakes are completely released. Spring-brakes on the trailer(s) can release more slowly than those on the power unit. In winter, brakes may freeze in the applied position. Driving with unreleased brakes for even a short distance can ruin tires beyond repair. If not fully released, a driveshaft brake can easily catch fire.

TRACTOR PROTECTION VALVE: To protect your power unit's air supply, every combination unit is equipped with a "tractor protection valve" that automatically activates when the power unit's pressure falls to a range of 45-20 psi to seal off the air lines between the power unit and the towed unit(s). When activated, this valve also dumps air pressure in the trailer air supply line and automatically applies the parking brakes on the trailer(s).

In an emergency, this valve can be operated manually by pulling the red octagonal knob located on the dash to cause an emergency application of the trailer parking brakes. **NOTE:** On older equipment, this valve might be manually activated by other means.

After hooking up to a trailer, push in the red knob to deactivate the tractor protection valve and insure that the trailer air system is charged. Activate the tractor protection valve during the pretrip inspection to be sure it is functioning properly.

Never activate the tractor protection valve knob to set the parking brakes. Always pull out the yellow diamond-shaped knob to set the parking brakes on the power unit and trailer. If the red knob also pops out automatically, both knobs must be pushed back in before you start to drive.

LOW-AIR PRESSURE WARNING DEVICES: In addition to a gauge, every air-braked vehicle must be equipped with a device to indicate when there is insufficient air pressure for proper operation of the brakes. Most vehicles are equipped with both an audible and a visible low-air warning.

If the low-air warning comes on while you are driving, stop the unit in the nearest safe location. Don't attempt to operate any farther until the air loss has been corrected. The low-air warning may not be activated by low air pressure in the trailer system alone. If the gauge pressure fluctuates without a brake application, or if pressure does not build to governor cut-out pressure (approximately 120 psi), check to be sure that the trailer air system is charged.

After parking, do not resume driving until the low-air warning(s) cease to operate and the gauge pressure reads at least 100 psi.

BLEEDING AIR TANKS: Air tanks should be bled at least once daily to remove moisture and sludge. This should be done before going off duty at the end of the day. Failure to bleed the tanks may lead to freezing of moisture in cold weather, which makes the brakes inoperative. Sludge will cause damage to internal components.

Allow each tank to drain completely. Close the drain cocks and rebuild air pressure to at least 100 psi before attempting to move the unit.

ANTILOCK BRAKE SYSTEMS (ABS): In March 1995, the National Highway Traffic Safety Administration (NHTSA) issued rules requiring antilock brake systems (ABS) for heavy trucks, tractors, trailers, and buses. Specifically these rules require ABS for:

- All new truck-tractors manufactured on or after March 1, 1997;

- All new air-braked trailers and single-unit truck and buses manufactured on or after March 1, 1998; and

- All new single-unit trucks and buses with hydraulic brakes manufactured on or after March 1, 1999.

The purpose of the antilock system is to control wheel lock-up, which can cause a vehicle to skid and possibly jackknife. This is accomplished by an electronic system which senses the speed of each wheel. When the wheel speed sensor detects an imminent lock-up a valve is opened and air in the chamber is released. As the wheel speed increases, the valve is closed and air is reapplied. All of this occurs automatically if the vehicle is stopping and a lock-up is sensed.

The antilock system activates when you apply pressure to the brake pedal sharply enough to lock the wheels. The computer system senses the potential for lock-up and "pumps" the brakes at a rate three to five times faster than a human could.

You should never pump the brakes when operating a vehicle with an antilock brake system. Let the computer do the work for you.

Most ABS-equipped vehicles have a warning light on the dashboard. This light will turn on for a few seconds when starting your vehicle. If the light stays on or suddenly turns on while you are driving, the ABS may not be working. Though you still have properly working brakes, the antilock function may not be working. Get this checked out as soon as possible.

The light also turns on for a short period of time when the brakes are applied.

ELECTRICAL PROBLEMS: Replace burned out lights at the earliest opportunity. If the unit is equipped with fuses, know where the fuses and fuse box are located, and how to make replacements.

If a circuit breaker buzzes, snapping the points open with your fingers may dislodge dirt and correct the problem. Check accessible wiring connections and tighten loose ones, if possible. Never let metal objects make contact across wiring connections. This may create a short circuit and damage the electrical system or start a fire.

ROAD FAILURES: Be sure you are familiar with company policy regarding breakdowns on the road. When you report a breakdown, provide as much information as possible about the cause. If you cannot determine the cause, describe the symptoms so that the person taking the call will have the best possible idea of the parts and tools necessary to correct the problem.

Record the breakdown on your Vehicle Condition Report. If you have repairs performed on the road, be sure the individual or shop doing the work signs the certification that repairs have been made. If the maintenance personnel decline, federal regulations allow you to sign the certification as the representative of the motor carrier.

If a condition develops that makes your unit unsafe to operate, or may result in major equipment damage, stop in the first safe place and contact the company before going further.

Notes